Prefabs
A social and architectural history

Acknowledgements

We want to thank all the prefab residents, past and present for their time, enthusiasm and generosity during the writing of this book.

Thanks are also due to those who saw the book through publication from start to finish including Clare Blick, John Hudson, Victoria Trainor and Nigel Wilkins from Historic England, and the following freelancers: Anne McDowall, for copyediting the text, Linda Elliott of Hybert Design, for the design layout, and Caroline Jones of Osprey Indexing, for providing the index.

1 | Introduction

The genesis of *Prefabs: A social and architectural history* has been our work with those who have lived, or are still living, in 'prefabs' – temporary homes built in factories at the close of the Second World War (Fig 1.1). As slums and bombed homes were cleared after the Blitz, there was a very real need for housing, and successive governments turned to prefabrication as a quick solution. These squat little homes with slightly pitched roofs, pretty gardens and all the mod cons became home to thousands of people around the country, often those who'd previously not had the luxury of hot running water or a fridge. No wonder, then, that they became so loved. They were meant to last just a decade – a mere stopgap as the country got back on its feet – but many of the prefabs are still standing, with residents often fighting to hold on to them.

Recognition of their architectural and social significance finally came when 16 prefabs in Wake Green Road in Moseley, a suburb of south Birmingham, were given Grade II listed status by Historic England in 1998, followed by six of the least-altered prefabs in the Excalibur Estate in Catford, south-east London, in 2009 (Fig 1.2).

Recent funding from the Heritage Lottery Fund has allowed us to create a digital archive, where we gather photographs, oral histories and locations of prefabs past and present, with the aim of making this as complete a depository of the history of temporary prefabs as possible.[1] There has been growing public interest in these fast-disappearing homes and the communities they fostered, and so the importance of recording their histories is keenly felt.

Although this book focuses on the temporary prefabs, it also charts the wider role that prefabrication has played in the history of British housing, paying particular attention to social housing and its developments during and after the Second World War. It also explores architectural innovation and imaginative design in the field of prefabrication, and clever solutions being put forward to solve the housing crisis of today.

Architecture's oldest new idea

To place the temporary prefabs in their wider setting, it is useful to look back at earlier examples of prefabrication, which has often been described as 'architecture's oldest new idea'. Prefabrication has long been with us in one form or another: from the ancient Romans and invading Normans, who brought with them pre-built wooden parts in order to quickly construct a fortress on these shores, to catalogues offering flat-packed houses for those in the far reaches of the British Empire and more recent experiments with panels produced in a factory setting.

In an ongoing search for quicker and more convenient ways to build homes, the preparation of building elements off site – whether in a carpenter's workshop or in a foundry – and their standardisation led to increasingly sophisticated, innovative and speedy building methods, helping Britain to prosper in its colonies. As early as the beginning of the 17th century, rudimentary prefabricated structures were being shipped to new settlements abroad. The fishing village of Cape Ann, Massachusetts, in the USA, is thought to be the first place to have received panelised-wood houses from England, in 1624.[2] By the 19th century, the export of pre-cut timber houses had become a thriving industry and had reached other parts of the Empire – from Australia to South Africa. These simple structures were used for hospitals, storehouses and homes.

One notable example is Henry Manning's 'portable colonial cottage' (Fig 1.3). In 1833, Manning, a London carpenter, built a wood-frame house for his son, who was emigrating to

Fig 1.3
Henry Manning Cottage. An advertisement for 'Portable Colonial Cottages' by Henry Manning appeared in the 27 November 1837 edition of the *South Australian Record*.

Australia. It became a prototype for dozens of other such houses to be shipped there in the following years. The cottages consisted of grooved wooden posts embedded and bolted into a continuous floor plate carried on bearers, while various wood panels to clad the frame came in standard sizes and were interchangeable. The cottage required no site work apart from the construction of a simple foundation. According to Manning, 'whoever can use a common bed-wrench can put this cottage up', and importantly, 'as none of the pieces are heavier than a man or a boy could easily carry for several miles, it might be taken even to a distance, without the aid of any beast of burden'.[3] The cottages became a commercial success, and Manning developed several models of varying size and cost.

The 19th century also saw an exploration of iron as a building material that could be applied to prefabrication. Already used to make standardised components, such as windows, beams and trusses that were then inserted into traditionally constructed buildings, cast iron – strong and versatile – was also used to create fully prefabricated structures, such as bridges, lighthouses and even ships.[4] It was also used for simple buildings for export, and a number of model portable iron houses were shown at the Great Exhibition in Hyde Park in 1851 as examples of industrial advancement and imperial achievement.[5]

Crystal Palace itself (Fig 1.4) was an enormous building of prefabricated cast-iron and wood components and standardised sheets of glass which was designed by Sir Joseph Paxton for the Great Exhibition. Its skeleton of iron columns supported a network of girders and was based on a 7.3m module of parts prefabricated in Birmingham. It took nearly 10 months to build, and after

Fig 1.4

Crystal Palace was built using prefabricated cast-iron and wood components. [© The Francis Frith Collection, 981]

the exhibition, the Palace was taken apart piece by piece and moved to an area of London that still bears its name.

The advent of corrugated iron in the early 1830s meant that lightweight iron sheets and panels could now be prefabricated off-site and used for walls, roofs and doors, while the process of galvanising made it even more durable (Fig 1.5). Corrugated iron played a significant role in the development of prefabrication: it was widely advertised for industrial building purposes at home and for export to the colonies as prefabricated iron cottages, houses and churches.[6]

As the colonies became better established and the export market receded at the end of the 19th century, prefabricated homes found a ready market in Britain. Firms such as Boulton and Paul in Norwich offered portable corrugated-iron flat-pack bungalows. They also provided customer support in the form of workmen who travelled by train with the client's flat-pack house and erected it on the chosen site in a matter of days. Some Boulton and Paul 'tin houses' are still standing today, including a number of 'tin tabernacles' (Fig 1.6) and a much-loved home, rescued from oblivion, in the small market town of Holt in North Norfolk.

Fig 1.5
A temporary, portable hospital hut at Netley Hospital with four nurses at the door, c 1900. [(c) Wellcome Library, London, licensed for reuse under creative commons.org/licenses/ by/4.0. Taken from http:// wellcomeimages.org/indexplus/ image/V0015643.html]

Fig 1.6
Great Moulton Chapel is typical of 'tin tabernacles' often found in East Anglia, Wales and the West Country. It is believed to have been supplied flat packed by the Norwich firm of Boulton and Paul for the price of £105 18s 0d. [Courtesy of Museum of East Anglian Life, Stowmarket]

Between the wars, larger disposable incomes and the search for country and seaside retreats led to the rise in the purchase of bungalows, some of which were prefabricated from wood or iron. These varied in size – from simple one-bedroom weekend bungalows to more intricate and grand affairs. The emerging 'bungalow towns', within easy reach by rail from major cities, became increasingly visible up and down coastlines as well as inland.[7] And until the 1947 Town and Country Act put an end to the practice, unprofitable agricultural land was sometimes partitioned into what became known as 'plotlands' (Fig 1.7). Here, working-class communities built simple structures or adapted railway carriages and caravans as retreats on cheaply bought land. Although amenities were scarce, a spirit of enterprise and self-sufficiency prevailed.[8]

In parallel to these developments in Britain, the Continent saw its own experiments with prefabrication; thanks to plentiful supplies of timber, the Scandinavian countries produced prefabricated buildings for their own colonies and military campaigns. As the American building industry developed in response to the needs of settlers of new territories and gold prospectors, prefabrication became increasingly common in the USA, too, especially with the advent of steam-powered saw mills and mass-produced nails, such as in boom-town Chicago, which became a major centre of the housing industry.[9] The USA also saw a rise in iron imports for the production of prefabricated iron houses, which were particularly popular during the Gold Rush.

Back in the UK, meanwhile, the advances of the Industrial Revolution meant that the populations of city centres continued to swell. In response, architects, engineers and industrialists interrogated the idea of prefabrication as a possible solution to their housing needs.

Fig 1.7
Plotlands houses, built in the 1930s, facing the beach in Jaywick, Essex. [© Elisabeth Blanchet]

2 | All change

Two features are of particular note in the story of 19th-century British housing: state intervention in the provision of housing for the working classes, and the expansion of towns and cities into low-density suburbs. The Industrial Revolution saw cities grow exponentially: labourers from the surrounding countryside came in droves in search of work, and populations multiplied. But working-class housing and quality of life were in a dire state and failing to keep up with the fast pace of industrial development. Workers and their families were largely confined to rented rooms in shared houses, so overcrowded slums with poor ventilation and sanitation became common. Meanwhile, from the 1820s, the middle classes began to move out of congested town centres into clean, comfortable and altogether more genteel suburbs. Their vacated properties were in turn filled by artisans and the better-off working classes, and many homes were subdivided for rent.

Throughout the 19th century, the approach to building legislation was rather piecemeal – and poorly enforced[1] – but in an effort to respond to the alarming problems of poor housing, the Public Health Act of 1875 required local authorities to implement building regulations, also known as bye-laws, which insisted that each house should be self-contained, with its own sanitation and water. The Act also set out building standards and introduced minimum street widths and healthier house layouts, which formalised the building of regulated parallel lines of terraced housing that are still a familiar sight in British towns today.

At the same time, philanthropic institutions and charitable trusts, such as the pioneering Peabody Trust (formed in 1862), were building rather austere but sanitary tenement blocks to accommodate the city works. It was hoped that these flats would be seen as workable blueprints that would encourage private builders and attract investors. Factory owners with a philanthropic bent also constructed model villages for their workers, such as Titus Salt's Saltaire in West Yorkshire, built in the 1850s to service the textile industry (Fig 2.1).

By the end of the 19th century, it was evident that this good work made only a small dent in the provision of housing and

Fig 2.1
Saltaire, Titus Salt's planned village, was built to get his workers away from the 'dark satanic mills' of Bradford to a place with more space and fresh air. [© Pauline E, licensed for reuse under creativecommons.org/licenses/by-sa/2.0. Taken from geograph.org.uk/p/2946696]

that a more concerted effort to clear slums and build new working-class homes would have to be made to alleviate miserable conditions. The Housing for the Working Classes Act of 1890 empowered local authorities to build houses as well as clear slums; local authorities were also responsible for rehousing at least half of the people displaced by slum clearance. The London County Council (LCC), for example, built high-density blocks of flats in the inner city, such as the Millbank Estate in Westminster, often as part of slum-clearance schemes. Completed in 1903, it provided flats for rent and was notable for its Arts and Crafts design. However, rents for these municipal homes were not subsidised, which kept them out of reach of lower-income households.[2]

By this time, engineers were beginning to make forays into prefabrication. John Alexander Brodie, a civil engineer and Liverpool town planner, was at the forefront of precast concrete construction and, in 1905, Liverpool saw the first prefabricated concrete block of flats, the Labourers' Concrete Dwellings, go up in Eldon Street (Fig 2.2). This pioneering multistorey block was demolished in 1964, but there is still a surviving example of the scheme, Walton Stables, at the corner of Rice Lane and Queens Drive.[3]

Fig 2.2
John Alexander Brodie's experimental houses in Eldon Street, Liverpool. Built from precast concrete in 1905, they were demolished in 1964.
[© Liverpool Record Office, Liverpool Libraries, CE770]

Garden cities

As a response to the rapidly industrialising cities and squalid living conditions, social reformer Ebenezer Howard set into motion the garden-city movement with his book *To-morrow: A Peaceful Path to Real Reform,* published in 1898.

Influenced by Edward Bellamy's utopian novel *Looking Backward* and social theorist Henry George's work *Progress and Poverty,* he envisioned zoned cities in which an urban centre is surrounded by housing, industry and then a generous green belt of farmland – making the garden city nearly entirely self-sufficient. Each of his garden cities would have no more than 32,000 inhabitants.[4] This vision entailed a melding of town and country, through which lives would be made healthy, while at the same time restraining unwieldy urban sprawl.

The following year, The Garden City Association was set up, and in 1902, Howard's book was republished with the new title of *Garden Cities of To-morrow*. As his ideas gained traction and he attracted enough influential supporters, it was possible to raise sufficient capital to find and purchase a suitable plot of land in order to test his ideas.[5] In 1903, a vacant site in Letchworth in Hertfordshire was chosen. Town planner and architect Raymond Unwin and his partner Barry Parker, both devotees of the Arts and Crafts movement who shared Howard's reformist ideals, were selected to be the garden city's planners and architects.

Unwin and Parker's vision for the garden city was functional but had a vernacular approach: harmonious materials were to be used and the site's topographical features were to be respected as much as possible. Tree-lined, curving roads and generous open spaces were planned, while housing was low-density and had open floor plans to let in plenty of sunlight. The project soon ran into financial difficulties, however. As a solution, an approach was made to John St Loe Strachey, the editor of *The Spectator*, who was known to be keen to slow the influx of agricultural workers into overcrowded cities. His proposal was to mount the Cheap Cottages Exhibitions of 1905 and 1907, held at Letchworth. Architects were invited to build cottages at a cost of £150 each.[6] The exhibitions attracted thousands of visitors, who were introduced to new building materials and concepts, one of which was prefabrication.

One of the most remarkable exhibited cottages was John Alexander Brodie's prefabricated house (Fig 2.3). The catalogue of the 1905 Cheap Cottage Exhibition describes Brodie's cottage:

> This system of building was originally designed by Mr Brodie with the special objective of providing a thoroughly sanitary and economical building, suitable in every way for the housing of the poorest classes displaced owing to the demolition of insanitary areas in Liverpool. The benefits of the system can be most fully obtained where the work to be carried out is on a considerable scale, and where approximate repetition in size of slabs is possible.[7]

This cottage, still standing today at 158 Wilbury Road, has Graded II* listing, and is one of the earliest examples of completely prefabricated reinforced concrete systems in Britain. Brodie's ideas and his prototype house can be seen as one of the precursors to the utopian vision of mass production and standardisation that became central to the thinking of urban planners of the following decades.

After Letchworth came Hampstead Garden Suburb (1906) and Welwyn Garden City (1919), which to greater or lesser extent realised Howard's original vision. Despite the dilution of his utopian ideals of independent new settlements – and an initial shortage of truly affordable working-class homes – Howard's theories set in motion new ideas around town planning, while Unwin and Parker's street and house designs went on to influence housing standards in Britain.

Fig 2.3 a & b (opposite) John Alexander Brodie's cottage for the 1905 Cheap Cottage Exhibition was constructed using interlocking reinforced concrete panels, floor and roofing elements, with the joinery assembled in situ. [© Liverpool Record Office, Liverpool Libraries, CE802 & CE828]

CONCRETE·COTTAGE
N̄T·LETCHWORTH·

SOUTH·
ELEVATION

EAST·
ELEVATION

NORTH·
ELEVATION

GROUND·
FLOOR·
PLAN·

FIRST·
FLOOR·
PLAN

WEST·
ELEVATION

SECTION·
A·B·

UPPER FLOOR CONCRETE COTTAGE FOR LETCHWORTH
ERECTED AT COBB'S QUARRY JULY 31 '06 NO- 828

Munitions workers' housing

The First World War saw a rapid increase in the need for munitions workers, and the question of where to house them had to be solved quickly. This led to the building of both temporary and permanent housing, which were a precursor to both the post-war building initiatives and to the temporary solutions implemented after the Second World War.

In Woolwich, south-east London, for instance, 1,300 homes were built for munitions workers at the Royal Arsenal, and the intention was that the houses would be of a superior quality that would serve in the post-war era too. To that end, what eventually became known as the Progress Estate, completed by December 1915, was built on 96 acres (39ha) of farmland according to garden-city principles: many of the roads curved with the contours of the land, and field boundary trees were retained where possible. Each of the terraced houses had three bedrooms, an indoor toilet and a big range for cooking as well as a garden.

The number of workers swelled from 10,866 in August 1914 to 73,571 in 1917, 25,000 of whom were women. 'Many new shops have had to be built and equipped and 31 canteens have been provided to assist in the provisioning of the workers', reported Dr Addison, the Minister of Munitions, on 28 June 1917.[8] The estate couldn't accommodate all the workers, so the Building Works Department of the Royal Arsenal constructed 1,500 temporary wooden and asbestos 'hutments' (Fig 2.4). These chalet-type houses remained in place until

Fig 2.4
The Building Works department of the Royal Arsenal erected 'hutments' to house the workers.
[© Bexley Local Studies & Archive Centre, 41_21]

Fig 2.9

The Sunspan House was exhibited at the Daily Mail Ideal Home Exhibition in 1934. [© Mr Glyn Edmunds, IoE UID: 431846]

The Ideal Home Exhibition

Founded in 1908 by the *Daily Mail*, the Ideal Home Exhibition (now Show) was envisaged as a publicity tool for the newspaper. Aimed squarely at the working and middle classes, who increasingly found themselves with surplus money that could be spent on home improvements, it soon became a vehicle for exhibiting much that was aspirational and forward-looking in the sphere of homemaking and lifestyle. Alongside new products and time-saving gadgets, the Exhibition regularly showed prefabricated houses in the interwar years, and even built a model village in 1921 to show 16 of the latest house-building techniques, which included a steel-frame system and standardised components. The show village, at Welwyn Garden City, is now known as Meadow Green and was a gift to the nation.[29]

In 1934, the exhibition displayed 'The Village of Tomorrow', built in the International Style. It showed the Sunspan House (Fig 2.9) – a frame-and-panel building designed for mass production by the modernist architect Wells Coates and his partner David Pleydell-Bouverie. Variations for cottages and three-, four- and five-bedroomed houses were exhibited, each to be positioned to make the most of daylight and provide simple, stylish and economic dwellings. They were marketed as suburban villas or seaside retreats – but only 15 were built.[30]

Germany

In the 1920s, influential architect and founder of the Bauhaus art school Walter Gropius was exploring the possibilities of prefabrication to fulfil his ideas of efficient construction. Using industrially prefabricated 'building-block' elements, he designed an ensemble of buildings for the Bauhaus teachers in Dessau in 1925, and a year later, was commissioned by the municipality to build a suburban estate of affordable working-class houses. He used precast concrete joists and prefabricated, inexpensive hollow slag-concrete blocks to create the Törten Estate (Fig 2.10), which consisted of 314 terraced houses with kitchen gardens.[31]

Gropius and his colleagues sang the praises of all that was machine-produced. Standardisation and functionalism, rather than ornamentation, was the key to effective factory-based production. Swiss architect Hannes Meyer, who succeeded Gropius as Director of the Bauhaus school, went even further: he was convinced that standardisation was the 'alphabet of socialist architecture' and most appropriate for a new type of classless society. He considered function to be more important than style: in his view, a building was 'neither beautiful nor ugly, just right or wrong'.[32]

Another German architect of note is Konrad Wachsmann. He was Chief Architect at Christoph und Unmack, the largest manufacturer of timber buildings in Europe, and it was here that his interest in panel-and-connector systems was first kindled. Wachsmann went on to develop an industrial prefabricated wood construction system for single-family houses in 1925, the most famous example of which is the summerhouse that belonged to Albert

Fig 2.10

Törten Estate, Dessau, Germany. The estate was designed by Walter Gropius as a solution for cost-effective mass housing between 1926 and 1928. [Architeckt Walter Gropius, 13 Sietö-Foto-Tenschert-Yvonne-2012 © Bauhaus-Siedlung Dessau-Törten]

Einstein in Caputh near Potsdam. He also exhibited timber houses at the Berlin Building Exhibition in 1931. After emigrating to the USA, Wachsmann dedicated his life to working on industrialised housing systems. He collaborated with Gropius but, despite his enormous efforts and inventiveness – Wachsmann took out nearly 100 patents for jointing and panel systems – and Gropius's reputation, their 'Packaged House' was not a commercial success: fewer than 200 were ever produced and sold.[33]

France

In France, the ideas of the influential Swiss–French architect Le Corbusier were novel and far reaching. Le Corbusier sought efficient ways to house large numbers of people in response to the urban housing crisis, and in 1915, he planned the Maison Dom-Ino (Fig 2.11). The house – intended for mass production – would be made of reinforced concrete, but would be versatile. The interior could be rearranged according to the needs and wishes of the occupants.

In his treatise *Vers une architecture* (translated in 1927 as *Towards a New Architecture*), published in 1923, Le Corbusier put forward the idea of a house that would be mass-produced, like a car or a ship, using advanced technology and engineering to provide homes for all. In one of the essays in the book, 'Mass Production Houses', he writes that the house is a 'machine for living in'. One such design, the Immeubles-Villas, provided a plan for high-quality, high-density, prefabricated urban dwellings (featuring a roof terrace, an ornamentation-free façade and horizontal windows for maximum natural light) that would, according to Le Corbusier, solve the housing problems of industrialised countries.

Le Corbusier's designs and ideas on urban living were profoundly influential during reconstruction after the Second World War, but he himself did not manage to fulfil his original mission: to design and build cheap factory-made houses for working people on a large scale.

At the same time, self-taught architect, designer and factory owner Jean Prouvé had been experimenting with folded sheet metal to produce furniture,

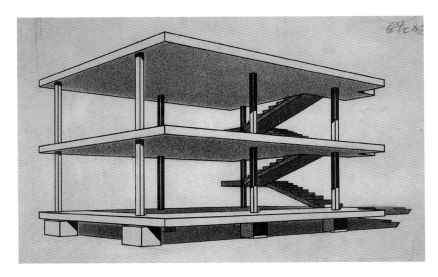

Fig 2.11
The Dom-Ino House was a standardised construction system designed by Le Corbusier for the reconstruction effort following the First World War. [© FLC/ADAGP, Paris and DACS, London 2017]

and eventually went on to develop architectural components such as moveable partitioning, metal doors and lift cages, as can be seen in the Maison du Peuple, a community centre in the Paris suburb of Clichy, which he helped to design in 1937. From the outbreak of the Second World War, his workshop produced emergency huts for soldiers, and after the war, this work evolved into an ambition to turn house building into a mechanised industry. His factory near Nancy produced houses (Fig 2.12), prefabricated huts (such as the 'Dismantable House'), doors, windows and façade panels.[34]

Fig 2.12

Jean Prouvé's 'Habitat Tropical', re-assembled at the Friche de l'Escalette, Marseille, 2016. [©Elisabeth Blanchet]

USA

In the USA, pre-cut building components that were assembled on site had been part of the construction industry since the early 19th century. Advances in the building industry meant that companies began to offer pre-cut houses that could be purchased through catalogues and assembled by the clients themselves. More than 100,000 Sears, Roebuck and Company's mail-order houses (Fig 2.13) were sold between 1908 and 1940, for example.[35] The homes came complete with all necessary materials, including nails and house paint, and there was little need to fear one's neighbour might end up with the same house as Sears produced nearly 450 different home types.[36]

The 1920s and 1930s saw a massive drive to experiment with prefabrication in order to provide low-cost housing. Materials such as concrete, plywood and steel were tried and tested – both by foundations especially set up for this research and by machinery industries that tried their hand at applying their knowledge to the production of affordable, mass-scale housing. Research was also carried out into low-cost heating methods and sanitation equipment.[37]

In 1933, as Roosevelt's New Deal created employment through public works, the Federal Government formed the Tennessee Valley Authority (TVA) to take charge of a dam development project at the Tennessee River basin. To house its workers and their families, the Authority built demountable, prefabricated homes. One of the first model communities was Norris, Tennessee, built in 1933. It was envisaged as a self-sustaining community with a green

Fig 2.13
Front cover of Sears, Roebuck and Co mail-order house catalogue. [Reproduced courtesy of Sears Holdings]

belt, based on the garden-city movement, and saw some architectural experimentation with wood and cinder blocks. Model communities, most of them temporary, continued to be built at all the TVA sites. The prefabs they showcased – simple kit houses equipped with modern amenities such as electricity, heating and indoor plumbing – were progressive for their time thanks to the work of Hungarian modernist architect Roland Wank, who was responsible for the design of six types of prefabricated house.[38]

Wank's houses (Fig 2.14) were simple and functional, with no mouldings, cornices or other ornamentation. He wrote:

Fig 2.14
A prefab home at Fontana Village, 1942. Like Norris Town, Fontana was built to accommodate workers during the construction of Fontana Dam in North Carolina.
[© Tennessee Valley Authority]

Frivolities like mouldings and cornices are not justified until we have attained utopia. Then, when we are all comfortably fixed, we shall sit down and wonder about the comparative merits of artistic detail. In the meantime, these ornaments express a desire to imitate what the financially able could afford in the more leisurely days of the past, and in that sense they are untruthful and needless.[39]

As the vast numbers of workers moved from one dam site to the next, their homes, which were made from plywood, produced off site and took very little time to construct, were dismantled and transported to their new locations. In all, the TVA produced 10,000 prefabricated units for its various projects.[40]

Czechoslovakia

The shoe factories and worker housing built by Tomáš Baťa in the small town of Zlín in the 1920s and 1930s were notable for their Functionalist architecture and garden city layout – although his factories were in the centre of town, rather than on the periphery as dictated by Ebenezer Howard. Baťa also built a cinema, numerous shops, canteens and a swimming pool for his workers. His business model was so successful that he exported it across the world, in particular to India and Africa but also to the UK. One of Baťa's notable satellites

Fig 2.15
Bata Hotel in East Tilbury, c 1937.
[Reproduced courtesy of the Bata Heritage Centre East Tilbury]

is in East Tilbury in Essex (Fig 2.15). Begun in 1932, the factory buildings were constructed with imported Czech steel girders (Zlín's architects had developed a reinforced-concrete frame that formed the basis for a wide range of company buildings, including factories), while the first houses used Czech designs and prefabricated fittings.[41]

USSR

Like many countries, the Soviet Union suffered a housing crisis between the two world wars. Equal housing for all was bound up in the ideology of the country, and architecture was regarded as an agent for profound social change. Standardisation, rationalisation and equal housing opportunities were the priorities of Soviet architects. In the late 1920s, Moisei Ginzburg, an influential Constructivist architect, developed modular housing using industrial materials, and designed, among other buildings, the Narkomfin 'semi-communal' block of flats in Moscow (Fig 2.16), whose interlocking apartments were a pioneering example of collective living.[42] Constructivist architects such as Andrei Burov and Boris Blokhin developed methods of building using prefabricated blocks and large panels. At the same time, other architects were experimenting with buildings made from entirely prefabricated dwelling units, a method that was replicated across Eastern Europe.

Fig 2.16
The Narkomfin building in Moscow, one of the most iconic examples of Soviet Constructivist architecture, built in 1930.
[© Robert Byron [Public domain], via Wikimedia Commons. Taken from https://commons. wikimedia.org/wiki/File:Robert_ Byron_1930s_Narkomfin_ building_(Architect_M._ Ginzburg).png]

THE NATION GIVES THANKS

VE VJ

1945
6 7 8 MAY
19 20 AUGUST
1995
DAY

VE·DAY VJ·DAY

WELCOM
HOM
HECT

3 The temporary prefab: An ideal home

To compound the ongoing problem of providing enough adequate housing, more than 200,000 homes were destroyed in Britain by enemy bombs during the course of the Second World War, and a great many more were severely damaged.[1] Many families that survived the bombardments between 1940 and 1945 were faced with homelessness, for which the country was poorly prepared. Emergency centres set up to deal with the problem could not cope, and many families had to rely on relatives and friends, or found themselves housed in Nissen huts or even forced to become squatters.

To cope with the increasingly desperate situation, Churchill's wartime Government had to come up with a solution not only to rehouse the homeless families but also to provide homes for returning servicemen. As the workforce and the materials for traditional house building were depleted, Churchill's War Ministry turned to a method that had been tried and tested in the interwar period: prefabrication.

Many still recall the squat bungalows that sprung up on brownfield land or on bomb sites in cities where once brick-and-mortar houses had stood (Fig 3.1). These snug, unassuming homes were delivered in separate parts, or even flat-packed from factories, and assembled in a matter of days or sometimes even just a few hours. Intended to last no more than a decade while the country got back on its feet, the prefabs became homes to many families in dire need. But despite their modest appearance, their design was progressive and technologically advanced, and the prefab estates followed the garden-city principles: curving roads, back and front gardens and plenty of light.

So what is so important about these humble homes? These 'palaces for the people', as one resident called them, capture a certain period in British history and are material evidence of strategic thinking at a time of need, original design and a real provision of care for the people of Britain. No wonder so many of their residents were so fond of them.

A quick solution

After the lacklustre outcome of the Homes Fit for Heroes initiative, the Government knew it couldn't let the people down again. Servicemen were expected to return to England in droves and many had higher expectations than after the Great War. Some had had access to education during their time in the army and aspired to a better standard of living. Moreover, after all they had given for their country, they expected a reward: a nice and comfortable house to come back to. The feeling was that 'It is up to those of us at home to see to it that all those who return find good houses for their families and themselves.'[2]

As early as 1941, the Conservative–Labour Coalition saw that rising costs meant that private building companies would struggle to provide sufficient affordable accommodation for rent. The Government therefore took on this responsibility and became a major supplier of homes for rent in the immediate post-war years. It fell to the Ministry of Works (MoW) to investigate what materials and skills would be needed by the building industry for the reconstruction of housing after the war, and it also considered non-traditional construction methods. In September 1942, the Government created the Interdepartmental Committee on House Construction, under the chairmanship of Sir George Burt, which soon became known as the Burt Committee. Burt gathered experts from the building industry, government departments and the Building Research Station.[3] The Committee's aim was 'to consider materials and methods of construction suitable for the building of houses and flats, having regard to efficiency, economy and speed of erection'.[4]

Meanwhile, the newly established Dudley Committee, set up by the Ministry of Health in 1942 – which represented the interests of the women's movement, local government, the construction industry and the medical profession – made a study of what the modern family expected from the interior layout of post-war housing. Having gained experience in the work place during the war, women would not tolerate indifferent conditions in their new homes.[5]

The Burt Committee requested local authorities and private enterprises to submit new ideas for non-traditional house design that could be put into production quickly. Each design of the hundreds submitted was inspected by a technical group, which decided whether a sample home should be built at the MoW's test ground in Northolt in West London.

In 1943, the Burt Committee was asked to expand its work to temporary housing solutions. Although some of its members were critical, claiming that temporary housing would consume vital resources needed for permanent construction, it became clear by the end of 1943 that only some form of quickly built temporary housing could alleviate the housing crisis. Aware of the work done by the Tennessee Valley Authority and other New Deal housing projects, the Burt Committee despatched a delegation of engineers to the USA to inspect the communities of demountable houses and site planning and to work with American architects from the TVA to come up with a design for temporary prefabricated houses that could be manufactured in America and shipped in pieces to Britain. In the end, the delegation recommended a design that was created by the Federal Public Housing Authority rather than the TVA. They called this house the UK100 (or the American), as it consisted of 100 wooden and Homasote (similar in composition to papier-mâché) parts and weighed

Burt and Mowlem

Sir George Mowlem Burt (1884–1964) followed his father's and uncle's path into the family firm, Mowlem, a large construction and civil engineering company. Contracts after the First World War included the Port of London Authority offices at Tower Hill, the Peter Robinson department store and various office buildings. From 1940 to 1945, Mowlem won more than £29 million worth of contracts, including airfield runways and concrete units for Mulberry harbours. Mowlem played an important role in post-war reconstruction, notably power stations and refineries. When Burt retired as chairman in 1961, his company ranked 11th in the British construction industry.[6]

just 8 tonnes. The first of an expected 30,000 UK100s (Fig 3.2) to be imported from the USA arrived in Britain in April 1945. Unfortunately, the end of the Lend-Lease Act (the means by which the USA aided its wartime allies with ammunition, raw materials and houses) saw this quota reduced to just 8,150.[7]

Fig 3.2
Dave Arnold's son in front of his family's prefab – a UK100 – in Clemson, South Carolina. Although made for export, some UK100 prefabs stayed in the USA and were used as houses on campuses such as the one in Clemson. [© Dave Arnold]

It was fortuitous that, as early as 1942, the Ministry of Aircraft Production was busy exploring ways in which it could branch out into prefabrication. A group of engineers and designers called the Aircraft Industries Research Organisation on Housing (AIROH) was formed to prepare a case for factory-produced housing and for the full use of the technical and scientific advances made in the aircraft industry during the war. At the same time, building company Tarran Ltd – which had gained experience of prefabrication during the interwar years – used Conway Hall in London to demonstrate that its prefabricated bungalow could be put up by 12 men in just nine hours.[8]

The Burt Committee's recommendation resulted in the Housing (Temporary Accommodation) Act of 1944 and the Emergency Factory Made Housing Programme, more commonly known as the Temporary Housing Programme. 'We felt that it was of the first importance that this project should not delay the building of permanent houses, and, consequently, that it should make the minimum demand on the building industry... The second object [...] is speed. We must have a scheme to meet urgent needs as quickly as possible, and that points to standardisation', said Henry Willink, the Minister of Health, in the House of Commons in 1944.[9]

As a result, a prototype of a steel and plywood Ministry of Works Emergency Factory Made House (also known as the 'Portal' or 'Portal's Palace', named after the then Minister of Works, Lord Wyndham Portal) was exhibited at the Tate Gallery in London from May 1944 (Fig 3.3). Designed by C J Mole, Deputy Director of MoW, it was a temporary one-storey house, envisaged for a life of 10 years and aimed at a family of four. It had a living room, kitchen,

bathroom, a separate toilet and two bedrooms. The kitchen was kitted out with a refrigerator, built-in cupboards and a foldable table, and the living room and bedrooms had clever storage solutions.

The Portal demonstrated how warm air could be carried by ducts from the living room fireplace to the bedrooms. It was put on display in order to gauge public and professional opinion and was visited by Churchill himself. *The Times* reported on 2 May 1944: 'It is hoped that as many women as possible, particularly working housewives and young married women, shall see the house.' The hope was, of course, to entice women back into the home after the war and to free up jobs for returning servicemen.

A prototype of the Portal was even exhibited at Kasr-El-Nil barracks in Cairo for the troops to examine the new type of home being built in the UK (Fig 3.4). 'The Egyptian climatic conditions... may make the House seem stuffy and the ceiling low, which would not be the case at home', warned a leaflet distributed at the exhibited prefab.

To test the livability of the Portal prototype, Albert Deighton, a civil servant at the Ministry of Works, who had been invalided out of the RAF, his wife Edith

Fig 3.4
A prototype of the Portal at
Kasr-El-Nil barracks in Cairo.
[© Imperial War Museum,
IWM H39466]

and their young son were invited to serve as trial residents. But before moving into the Portal prefab in November 1944, Albert had to sign the Official Secrets Act; he was not permitted to receive personal visitors or to discuss any aspect of the house with the press. Albert, who had been living with his wife's family, was pleased to finally get his own home, although its primary purpose was to serve as a show house.[10]

Despite the Portal being furnished with Utility furniture (*see* p 38) and fully kitted out 'down to the last teaspoon',[11] the Deightons discovered a number of problems with the prefab. As winter set in, boiling a kettle would lead to condensation running down the steel walls and freezing and the excessive damp caused mould to grow on items stored in the steel cupboards. News of this eventually made its way into the press and Albert was initially blamed, although his name was eventually cleared.

Although people were impressed by all the mod cons – 'Built-in fittings dazzle in comparison with their complete absence in the average council house'[12] – there was still some uncertainty from the public. One viewer called the Portal prototype a 'damn tin can',[13] architects and engineers sent numerous suggestions to the *Architects' Journal* regarding the prototype's layout and ceiling height, and *The Times* said, 'There is no getting away from the fact that the present exterior is dull and unpleasing'.[14]

A revised model of the Portal, taking in structural and technical amends such as the addition of a back door, was exhibited at the Tate Gallery a few months later. However, the shortage of steel and plywood made the Portal's production in quantity impossible – the price tag was just too high. Instead, as Churchill was so keen on this prefab, manufacturers were asked to use it as a prototype, and three other designs were selected and also exhibited at the Tate Gallery in 1944: the Uni-Seco (made of asbestos cement on a timber frame), the Tarran (concrete panels on a timber frame) and the Arcon (asbestos cement on

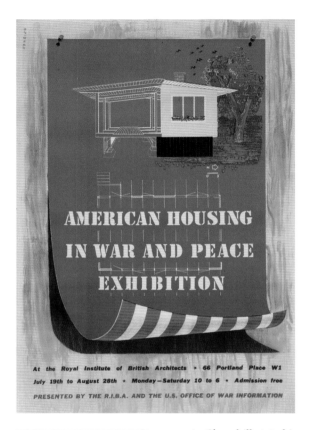

AMERICAN HOUSING
IN WAR AND PEACE
EXHIBITION

At the Royal Institute of British Architects • 66 Portland Place W1
July 19th to August 28th • Monday—Saturday 10 to 6 • Admission free
PRESENTED BY THE R.I.B.A. AND THE U.S. OFFICE OF WAR INFORMATION

Fig 3.5
The exhibition poster for
'American Housing in War and
Peace', held at the Royal Institute
of British Architects in London,
1944. [© Imperial War Museum,
Art.IWM PST 9542]

a light steel frame). The Aluminium was added in the summer of 1945. Albert was even allowed to move out of his damp Portal and into the Uni-Seco in the grounds of the Tate.[15]

To counter any remaining doubts, the Government actively promoted the prefabs: their virtues were sung – and any faults downplayed – in radio broadcasts, exhibitions and public discussions. The 1944 exhibition 'American Housing in War and Peace' (Fig 3.5), held at RIBA, showed aspirational American designs and attracted considerable interest, especially from the British architectural press. The message to the public was loud and clear: mass-produced housing, when well designed and made, would make for comfortable and tasteful homes. Further prefab prototypes were exhibited near Selfridges in London, and in other cities, such as Edinburgh.

The Temporary Housing Programme

The 1944 Temporary Housing Act authorised the expenditure of £150m to build prefabricated homes. Ten different types of prefabs (*see* pp 94–102) were manufactured under the Temporary Housing Programme and dispatched to cities most in need of emergency housing. As Churchill stated in a speech in 1944:

Factories have been assigned, the necessary set-up is being made ready, materials are being earmarked as far as possible, the most convenient sites [for the prefabs] will be chosen, the whole business is to be treated as a military operation handled by the government with private industry harnessed to its service. And I have every hope and a firm resolve that several hundred thousand of our young men will be able to marry several hundred thousand of our young women and make their own four-year plan (Fig 3.6).[16]

Although the manufacturing of prefabs faced criticism, the Government pushed ahead because the policy offered a number of clear benefits. Factories set up for war-time production would continue to function, workers would continue to find employment, and skilled builders would be released to concentrate their efforts on permanent housing and repairs. When the programme was first put forward, it was estimated that the standardisation of parts and the fewer man-hours needed to put up the prefabs would reduce the cost – the aim was to keep the cost at £550 per bungalow (around half that of a traditionally built house at the time).[17] Moreover, the inclusion of items such as a refrigerator and a gas cooker were meant to stimulate the post-war economy: if tenants got used

Fig 3.6
The Bazell family in front of their
prefab in North London, 1950s.
[© The Prefab Museum]

to these luxury items, they were more likely to purchase them for themselves once they were allocated permanent housing. 'I remember my mother was absolutely thrilled to have the things that others didn't: a refrigerator, a boiler for the washing, all the cupboards – everything under one roof', recalls Valerie Sommerville (Fig 3.7), who spent her childhood on the Excalibur Estate in Catford, which consisted of 186 Uni-Seco prefabs and was one of the largest such estates in the country.[18]

Fig 3.7
Valerie Sommerville outside her
childhood prefab on the Excalibur
Estate. [© Elisabeth Blanchet]

The prefabs were constructed of pre-built panels, either attached to a prefabricated wood or metal frame or built of self-supporting prefabricated panels, produced in factories. Churchill had hopes for half a million such homes. (Fig 3.8) The Ministry of Works contracted construction firms to erect the houses and make a garden path and fencing, while local authorities obtained sites and prepared off-site services and roads. Maintenance and repairs then became the responsibility of the local councils, who arranged the lettings. 'The authority will choose the tenants, fix and receive the rents, manage the property and keep it in repair. The authority will make an annual payment to the Ministry of Health of an amount to be determined', dictated the official instruction manual.[19]

Fig 3.8
Ceremony marking the erection of the 100,000th temporary house in the UK, at Wandsworth, South London, in 1947.
[P_H00132_001]

It was up to local authorities to decide where prefabs would be erected. Occasionally, prefabs were used to replace bomb-damaged homes and fill the holes in a street between traditional houses. Such was the case in the London areas of Peckham, Nunhead, Dulwich, Elephant and Castle and Shoreditch, for example (Fig 3.9). Estates of prefabs (from 50 units to hundreds) also popped up on brown and greenfield sites and on vacant and derelict land in cities and in rural areas. Even unlikely places such as cemeteries were put to this use.

Fig 3.9
A Uni-Seco prefab 'filling in' where a bomb was dropped on Inverton Road, Nunhead, South London, 2003. [© Elisabeth Blanchet]

The prefab kitchens featured a gas or electric cooker, a gas fridge, space-saving built-in cupboards, a folding-down table and a 'copper', a large metal bowl under which a gas flame could be lit to heat water for washing clothes (Fig 3.14).

Féjer's designs were used in all the prefabs, and when the Women's Group on Public Welfare – a voluntary organisation concerned with the welfare of women and children – published a report on the effect of the temporary prefabricated bungalow on household routines in 1951, it found that, despite low ceilings and complaints about keeping the prefab warm, the modernity of the kitchen and bathroom, sensible plumbing and the large windows were the main reasons for women's overall satisfaction with the prefabs.[24]

Fig 3.14
Excalibur resident Ted Lawson in his Uni-Seco prefab kitchen in 2005. [© Elisabeth Blanchet]

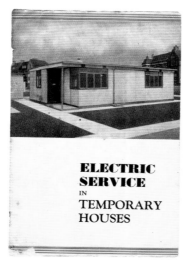

Fig 3.15
Electric Service in Temporary Houses, the instruction manual published by the British Electrical Development Association and issued to new residents of prefabs. [© The Prefab Museum]

Electricity

Just after the war, about a quarter of the British population didn't have mains electricity supply, so the Electrical Development Association (EDA) produced a booklet, *Electric Service in Temporary Houses*, to enable new residents to take advantage of the efficiency and freedom electricity could bring to their lives. Each prefab had six electric power points: two in the kitchen, two in the living room and one in each bedroom. In the kitchen, the cooker was more advanced than those most people had been used to: it had an oven, a separate grill, two hotplates and a SIM control for simmering. All the instructions on how to use it were also given in the booklet (Fig 3.15).

Another revolutionary item was the gas-powered refrigerator, a luxury that few residents could have afforded previously. It had the capacity of three cubic feet, a volume that the EDA manual considered 'ample for the storage of perishable food needed for an average household'. The residents were advised to use it all year long, not only in the summer.

Heating

In the early prefabs, the only source of heat was provided by a coal fireplace. A back boiler heated water that was then stored in a tank in the airing cupboard. In some types of prefabs, ducting pumped hot air from the fireplace to the bedrooms, but it wasn't particularly effective, and most residents complained about the prefabs being stuffy in summer and freezing and damp in winter. Sometimes, the door of the oven would be left open to help heat the prefab.

'I remember it was so cold during the winter; there was just a tiny fireplace. Every night, I used to put cloths on the windows and they'd freeze solid. In the bedrooms, the walls used to go green with damp', reminisces Joyce Cramp, who has lived in her Killamarsh (North Derbyshire) Tarran prefab since 1955.[25]

Furnishing the prefabs

In 1944, Churchill had claimed that 'They [the emergency houses] are, in my opinion, far superior to the ordinary cottage as it exists today. Not only have they excellent baths, gas or electric kitchenettes and refrigerators, but their walls carry fitted furniture – chests of drawers, hanging cupboards and tables which today it would cost eighty pounds to buy.' Moreover, he promised that, 'for the rest of the furniture, standard articles will be provided and mass produced so that no heavy capital charge will fall upon the young couples or others who may become tenants of the houses'.[26]

However, although the prefab came with in-built cupboards, a drop-down table in the kitchen and some even had a drop-down ironing board, many of the residents had lost everything in the Blitz so life remained quite tough for some time. 'I remember we didn't have much furniture and no carpet in the prefab, so my grandmother went out and bought grey surplus Army blankets, machined them together in a quilted pattern and put green bindings on the edges, and we had these carpets in the bedroom', recalls Valerie Sommerville, who lived on the Excalibur Estate.[27]

Rationing, the lack of skilled labour and a shortage of timber and plywood, much of which was redirected to the war effort, created a scarcity of new furniture during the war. Although prices for furniture were regulated, quality often varied, so the solution was to standardise the design and material of newly produced pieces. To assist young couples in setting up their homes (about half a million marriages took place during every year of the war), the Government set up the Utility Furniture Scheme in 1942. A Utility Furniture Advisory Committee was established, which appointed Gordon Russell, a champion of accessible, well-crafted design with a background in the Arts and Crafts movement, to oversee furniture production 'to ensure a supply of furniture of the best quality available at controlled prices to meet a real need'. Two consumer representatives were also part of the committee: Reverend Charles Jenkinson and Mrs E Winborn, who represented 'the ordinary housewife'.[28] In October

Fig 3.19
The world-record-holding team
who put up an AIROH within
41 minutes in Whitehawk,
Brighton during November 1946.
[© The Prefab Museum)

An ideal garden

Each prefab had a front and back garden and it didn't take new residents long to start using this new-found space to grow fruit and vegetables. The wartime 'Dig for Victory' campaign was still on everybody's minds and growing their own produce was necessary to balance the ration restrictions that were maintained after the war. In 1947, bread and potatoes were rationed for the first time. Many supplemented their diets with apples, raspberries, gooseberries, loganberries, strawberries and blackcurrants grown in their back gardens. For those unfamiliar with gardening, help was at hand in the form of guides such as *How To Grow Food*, published to help people adapt to wartime and the post-war period.[39]

Meanwhile, the Women's Voluntary Service (WVS) Garden Gift Scheme (Fig 3.20) began in April 1946 to brighten and smarten up newly built prefabs, which often stood on little more than barren building sites or land only very recently cleared of bomb debris. Through the scheme, WVS volunteers collected plants and seeds from donors, often in the countryside, and delivered them to new residents. The scheme was taken up with such enthusiasm that a prefab garden, exhibited by the Women's Voluntary Service, featured at the Chelsea Flower Show every year from 1947 to 1955. The WVS prefab garden exhibits included a replica prefab house made from felt and stucco and the approximate amount of land usually allotted to a house. The exhibits aimed to demonstrate to the visitors the best way to gain the most from the small amount of space, while showing how the gardens could be used as a means of self-sufficiency.

Fig 3.20
This poster, one of very few surviving from the late 1940s, reflects the nature of the Garden Gift Scheme, presenting a stylistic departure from the war years: gone are the stark warnings and calls to arms; in their place are stylised flowers and friendly words. [Courtesy of Royal Voluntary Service]

The model prefab garden was planted with all manner of flowers, along with a vegetable patch that included a collection of herbs, which, during the times of rationing, really drew interest from the crowds. These exhibits proved to be a tremendous success and helped spread the word about the Garden Gift Scheme. And in 1949, the Queen Mother even sheltered in the prefab when an inopportune rainstorm hit the Flower Show.

Visiting prefab gardens was very much part of the royal calendar. On 30 July 1947, Princess Elizabeth visited bombed areas in south-east London with officials of the London Gardens Society. 'She particularly admired the prize-winning garden of Mr W C Bodger, a railway foreman, and asked if she might inspect his prefabricated house', reported the *Illustrated London News* on 9 August 1947. Queen Mary was a particular champion and the Queen Mother often visited prefab gardens in London. The WVS even ran a competition, offering a silver trophy presented by Queen Mary for the best prefab garden.

By 1948, it was estimated that at least 15,000 homes had been helped in the London area alone through this scheme, and the idea had spread to 28 other towns and cities across the country.[40]

On 18 January 1949, Dorothy de Rothschild, from the Homes and Gardens Department of the WVS, wrote to *The Times*: 'This scheme has brought us into close contact with thousands of tenants of temporary housing estates who had never had any previous opportunity for gardening. Owing to the encouragement brought by a tangible gift, many householders have planted their gardens and have been surprised and thrilled to see them flourish.'

By the early 1950s, with the fear of rationing diminishing, prefab tenants converted parts of their garden into a play area for children or into flowerbeds for roses. Slowly, front gardens became lawns and flowerbeds, a sure sign of social stability (Fig 3.21). Gardening became a shared hobby among prefab

Fig 3.21
Front garden of the AIROH prefab at St Fagans National Museum of History, 2013. [© Elisabeth Blanchet]

residents (Fig 3.22). The estate layouts, with footpaths, alleys and low fences, encouraged people to look at the neighbours' efforts and there was certainly a healthy sense of competition. Best garden layouts and flowerbeds garnered prizes (Fig 3.23), and residents were not shy about decorating their green spaces with wishing wells and gnomes.

Fig 3.22

Back garden of the AIROH prefab at St Fagans National Museum of History, 2013. [© Elisabeth Blanchet]

MAYOR'S PARLOUR
LEWISHAM TOWN HALL
LONDON SE6 4RU
☎ 01-690 4343

11th July 1985

Mayor
COUNCILLOR *MARGARET SANDRA*

Dear Mr. O'Mahoney,

    May I offer my congratulations for your success in the Prettiest Front Gardens Competition. I much appreciate your work in making the Borough a more pleasant place to live in.

Yours sincerely,

Mayor

Mr. E.J.J. O'Mahoney
6 Persant Road
SE6

Fig 3.23

Lewisham's mayor congratulated Eddie O'Mahony on his win in the 'Prettiest Front Gardens Competition' in 1985. [© The Prefab Museum]

Prefabs for export

Curiously, even though social housing was still in short supply in Britain at the end of the 1940s, almost 2,000 temporary prefabs were sold by the Government for £150 each and exported all over the world (three quarters to Australia, where they helped to house immigrants).[41] The decision to export the prefabs was part of an export trade that helped to pay for supplies of meat and wool, for example. The prefabs also encouraged emigration to under-populated parts of the Commonwealth. For example, in 1946, the Labour Government authorised a massive peanut-growing operation in Tanganyika (now Tanzania) to produce cooking oil for export. Ex-soldiers volunteered to grow the nuts, but at first there was no housing, so 50 prefabs were shipped there to accommodate the workforce.[42]

In 1949, Ernest Kinghorn, Labour MP for Great Yarmouth stated in the House of Commons:

> I am certain that we have enough experience in this country to give a great boost to sending houses to all parts of the Colonial Empire. We could help not only the Colonies but also ourselves, because the supply of these prefabricated houses could be regarded as part of our exports. We could export thousands of houses specially made for tropical territories in Africa and Australia. I hope this suggestion will be considered in the near future when the Prime Ministers of the Commonwealth countries come here for discussions with our political leaders.[43]

The concern with housing in the colonies was not unique to Britain. French architect and designer Jean Prouvé designed and manufactured three prototype Maisons Tropicales for France's African colonies between 1949 and 1951. His Brazzaville house, for example, was made from folded sheet steel and aluminium and, for ease of transport, all its components were flat, lightweight and could be neatly packed into a cargo plane. Prouvé designed for the demands of the climate and included a veranda with an adjustable aluminium sun-screen. The inner walls were made of fixed and sliding metal panels, with blue glass portholes to protect against UV rays, while a double roof structure was produced natural ventilation. Although designed for mass-production, the prototypes proved no less expensive than locally built buildings so they remain as unique examples of Prouve's experiments.

Life in the Orlits on the Isle of Dogs

Pat Jarvis

By the time I was nine, my oldest sister was 12 and, as we only had two bedrooms, it was getting a bit overcrowded, so my mum contacted the Council and we were offered a three-bedroom Orlit house. We were so excited because we had two gardens, front and back, and inside and outside toilets. I remember the first time I walked in the front door – it was 1968 – it looked enormous to me. There was a flight of stairs to the right, and straight in front was the door to the kitchen. There was a big glass door to the back garden opposite the kitchen door, and the cooker and sink to the right, with two small worktops and lots of cupboards underneath. On the left-hand side of the kitchen was a doorway and a sliding hatch with worktops and low-level and overhead cupboards, with a tall larder in the corner. At the left side of the back room, there were big wooden-framed folding doors that led into the sitting room – or, as we called it, the front room. We would slide them open in the summer to help to cool the house. They were heavy and a bit stiff to slide back and forth, but in the winter they helped to keep the front room warm. As there wasn't any heating downstairs apart from an open fire, it was always cold downstairs. I lived in our Orlit house for nine years until I left home to become a nurse.[15]

Orlits consisted of a structural precast-concrete frame clad in small precast reinforced-concrete panels, and had a flat roof. The site work was largely a matter of fitting together ready-made components. Both Orlit houses and flats had a living room, kitchen, three bedrooms, bathroom and WC. Cookers and wash-boilers were provided as part of the equipment of each dwelling, and slightly higher rents were charged because of this.[16] The Scottish branch of the company constructed Orlits in Scotland. By the 1980s, however, it became clear that the concrete in the Orlits had deteriorated to such an extent that the homes were designated as defective under the Housing Defects Act of 1984 and the majority of the 17,000 Orlits built have now been demolished.

The permanent AIROH

Although a two-storey design was at first considered for the permanent AIROH, engineers eventually developed a new house type using panel components, rather than a finished box structure like the temporary AIROH. The new bungalow – also known as the BL8 – was designed for site assembly. It had three bedrooms and was roomier than its temporary sibling. The homes were built as semi-detached or terraced and had shallow pitch gable roofs covered in aluminium sheets. The structure was a lightweight, recycled-aluminium frame and the external walls were of corrugated aluminium sheeting, lined internally with plasterboard, with glass-fibre insulation in the cavity. The houses were manufactured by A W Hawksley Ltd and the Bristol Aeroplane Company and 17,000 were built between 1948 and the mid-1950s. The permanent AIROH houses were sold to local authorities at extremely favourable rates, but on the condition that they went to areas with an industrial labour shortage. For example, 250 bungalows were allocated to Bilborough in Nottingham, where they were assigned to miners in order to encourage the mining area to increase coal production in the post-war years.[17]

Life in a BL8 bungalow in Redditch

Nina and Alan Mason (Fig 4.5)

Nina: They were bitterly cold at first. The only heating you really had was in the front room. You had to go to bed with two or three layers on. I enjoyed growing up in the prefab. I still like the prefabs, they are very nice, especially for people with disabilities. They are probably even the best accommodation in Redditch at the moment, really, especially if you have a wheelchair.

Alan: These homes were built in 1950/1951. Each one took about a week to construct. They are called BL8 and were built in Gloucester using the metal from old fighter planes that had been shot down. People have misconceptions about prefabs. They think they are old and draughty and falling down, but they're not. The gardens are very big. There's plenty of room for us; plenty of room for parties, if you want them. In 2001/2002, the local authority wanted to pull down the prefabs on our street, but we fought and won. We got £750,000 from the Council to refurbish the prefabs: we got new walls and new roofs.[18]

Fig 4.5

Nina and Alan Mason in their BL8 Aluminium bungalow in Redditch. [© Elisabeth Blanchet]

The Wates

During the war, construction company Wates Ltd built aerodromes, army camps, factories, and, most notably, developed precast and in-situ reinforced-concrete barges and floating docks. The company supplied major parts of the Mulberry Harbours that were towed across the Channel after D-Day. After the war, Wates used its knowledge of precast concrete to build more than 60,000 houses and flats. Its system was based on a 12in (30cm) module that consisted of panels cast in metal moulds with provision for windows where necessary. Inside, the houses (Fig 4.6) were fitted with prefabricated panels to reduce working time on site.[19]

Fig 4.6

The Wates house [AA98_06364]

Airey houses

The Airey system (Fig 4.7) was designed by the Leeds industrialist and builder Sir Edwin Airey as early as 1925. The homes required precast concrete blocks, small enough to be handled by one or two men, which were made in nine factories, one of which was Airey's own factory in York. There were two variants: the urban version had a flat roof, while the rural version had a steeply pitched gable roof. The weatherboarding effect, along with conventional pitched roofs, was intended to make the prefabs look like traditional homes. About 26,000 Airey homes were built in the period up to 1955, often by local contractors, who could purchase sections from factories with the help of a government subsidy.[20]

Fig 4.7
An urban type of the Airey
House, one of the most prolific
of permanent prefab designs,
being erected by London County
Council. [P_H00005_004]

A pair of Aireys could be built in two weeks and their construction did not require skilled labour or any special equipment.

The Cornish Unit

Developed by the English China Clay Company in Cornwall, the Cornish Unit houses (Fig 4.8) were built from units using concrete in which the aggregate was fine sand, the waste material from china clay pits. The designs were finalised by 1946 and more than 40,000 homes were built by local authorities across the country in the following 10 years. These homes have distinctive reddish-brown mansard roofs and were built as bungalows, two storey semi-detached and terraced houses.[21]

The Howard House

Designed by Frederick Gibberd and produced by civil engineering and building contractors John Howard & Co, the Howard House (Fig 4.9) was suitable for mass production in factories. It was made with a light steel frame, clad with asbestos panels and lined with fibreboard with aluminium foil insulation. It had a three-way adaptable plan and took just a few days to erect. The kitchen was delivered to the site as a finished unit with all its fittings ready to be connected. Only 1,500 were built.

Fig 4.8
The Cornish Unit [DP172145]

Fig 4.9
Howard House, designed by
Frederick Gibberd, being erected.
[OP33568]

Imported prefabs

The densely forested Scandinavian countries had long been highly adept at timber prefabrication. Sweden was the most prolific, and by the beginning of the 20th century, Stockholm was leasing plots of land so blue-collar workers could construct their own homes using a standard plan provided by the city. The prefabricated industry developed quickly, and by the 1930s, more than 20 manufacturers were offering 'catalogue homes'.[22] The emphasis was on standardised parts rather than standardised houses, which avoided uniformity. By the end of the war, Sweden was exporting prefabs to Finland and Norway.

On 16 June 1945, the *Illustrated London News* reported that 5,000 prefabricated timber homes had been purchased from Sweden (Fig 4.10). A mission had been sent to Stockholm by the then Minister of Works, Duncan Sandys. The houses ordered were of two types, suitable for urban or rural living, and all were of two-storey design, detached or semi-detached, and included two or three bedrooms, a living room, bathroom, outside wash-house, a fuel room and a store room. The design was adapted by the Ministry of Works from a standard all-timber Swedish kit (they are often called 'kit homes') and the houses arrived in flat-packed sections.

Most of the Swedish houses went to rural areas with poor housing provision. For example, 30 Swedish houses were allocated to Loddon Rural District Council in south Norfolk. Built to withstand Nordic conditions, they were also a good fit for Scotland – 2,500 were built in 1945 and another 1,000 added in 1949.[23] They were scattered all over Scotland: a hundred such houses were built in two locations in Edinburgh, some went to areas near Glasgow and hundreds more were erected in the Hebrides and Orkney.

Although young and leading architects were excited by the potential of prefabrication, there was little concerted effort to develop the aesthetic of the permanent prefabs beyond expectations of what a 'traditional' house ought to look like. What is more, although they did provide a service in terms of

Fig 4.10
In the mid-1940s, Sweden exported 5,000 prefabricated houses to England and 2,100 to France. The first of these houses was built at Abbots Langley, Hertfordshire, in January 1946. [P_H00002_004]

implementing unconventional materials and offering labour-saving techniques in times of austerity, they were often more expensive to build than conventional homes. Local authorities tended to place them on the outskirts of cities, as they were inadequate to satisfy the housing needs of overpopulated inner cities. In the end, architects concerned with rebuilding Britain after the war decided that the answer must lie not in a traditional cottage but in something more ambitious. By the mid-1950s, large precast concrete panels were becoming cheaper to manufacture. They were best applied to medium and high-rise blocks of flats. The era of the high-rise was born.

Life in a Swedish House in South Harris, Scotland

Kenna Morrisson (Fig 4.11)

I loved the house straight away and I immediately 'booked' my bedroom. It used to have a fireplace; that's why I picked it. We used it a lot, and I remember using it when my own children were born, too. The chimney in the living room was quite high. It had an oven down below and it had a wee hot plate, which was just great. You could bake on it. My favourite thing to do on the hot plate was pancakes.

Fig 4.11

Kenna Morrisson still lives in the Swedish House in Leverburgh, South Harris, Scotland, that was allocated to her father in 1947. [© Elisabeth Blanchet]

I remember when the houses were assembled; I was 13. They arrived by boat. They were all gutted and refurbished in the early 1990s. We lost a lot of practical cupboards in the kitchen. The local authorities thought about demolishing them and building new houses. All the tenants were asked if they wanted to go to the new houses or stay here but most of us didn't want to move. They are such landmarks.[24]

5 | Vertical cities

To be sure, the vast quantities of temporary and permanent prefabs helped alleviate the demand for social housing in the post-war years, but inner-city slum housing remained a pressing issue. In 1954, Harold Macmillan announced a mass drive for slum clearance, which fell largely on local-authority shoulders, and during the next two decades, some 1.2 million pre-1914 homes were demolished in England and Wales.[1]

Urban populations were rapidly growing, due to a post-war baby boom, and house waiting lists were ballooning, so local authorities had to build, and they had to do it fast. They had the power to compulsorily purchase inner-city land for clearance and redevelopment. Demolition paved the way for young architects and city planners who had come to professional maturity in the inter-war and post-war years and were heavily influenced by the European modern movement and the thinking of Le Corbusier. They could redesign town centres in a drive to rebuild and 'reorder' Britain into a modern and more equal society. As Miles Glendinning and Stefan Muthesius put it in their work on modern public housing, 'Modern design simply meant the spirit of comprehensive renewal, the search for the New, through scientific investigation as well as verbal and visual rhetoric'.[2] The technology and opportunity had arrived for modernist architects to realise Le Corbusier's utopian urban vision of 'vertical cities' for the masses, where people would live in high-rise 'neighbourhoods' with a full range of facilities and amenities. The new high-rise tower blocks, some of which relied heavily on prefabrication, presented a swift solution to the problem of urban overcrowding, and London County Council (LCC) was at the forefront of their design and construction.

The only way is up

From 1956, central-government subsidies were made available for multi-storey developments and were formulated so as to increase in accordance with the height of the building. By then, reinforced concrete had become a reliable and easy-to-source material for construction. Building parts were precast in factories before they were assembled onsite, and the building of flats was facilitated in the early 1950s by the introduction of tower cranes, which could lift weights of about 30 tonnes. The newly devised 'box-frame' method of construction, where individual cells, or rooms, were set horizontally and vertically together to create an overall structural frame, lent itself to repetition and standardisation, and therefore to faster construction times. Building with large precast concrete panels followed in the 1960s (Fig 5.1). The rapid construction of tower blocks relied on large-scale contractors establishing factories across the country that prefabricated concrete frames and panels, either to their own system or ones used on licence from Europe.

Fig 5.1
Park Hill estate in Sheffield was completed in 1961 and regarded as a perfect expression of a utopian vision of social housing.
[DP030885]

By 1965, 163 developers were producing 138 different large-panel systems (LPS) for housing. One of the most common was the Bison Wall-Frame method used by Concrete Ltd. Here, all walls were load bearing; the walls and panels were 21 feet (6.4m) long, and a two-bedroom flat could be completed from just 21 precast components. This method also allowed for a completely prefabricated bathroom and unit to be slotted in.[3] The largest LPS scheme in London was the Aylesbury estate of 2,700 flats that was built by contractor Laing between 1967 and 1977. Taylor Woodrow, meanwhile, favoured the Danish system Larsen Nielsen, an example of which can be found at Kedge House in North Millwall in London. Built in the late 1960s, it is a flat-roofed, 10-storey block of 40 one-to-four bedroom flats faced with concrete aggregate panels.[4]

Architects championed 'streets in the sky' – wide internal walkways built outside flats to give children places to play. They sat above the level of cars, and the rise in road-traffic accidents made the idea of pedestrian walkways popular. A prime example is the ambitious Park Hill estate in Sheffield, completed in 1961, which was regarded as the perfect expression of a utopian vision of social housing (see Fig 5.1). Intended to mimic the communal nature of the back-to-back houses it replaced, it was equipped with many of the facilities of a small town, including a butcher's, a dressmaker and four pubs. Its 995 flats were arranged around 'street decks' wide enough for a milk float.

From prefab to high-rise

Sarah Drinkwater, East Acton

My parents, brother and I moved into an AIROH B2 prefab in 1955 when I was 18 months old. It was on quite a large estate of prefabs in East Acton, London. We loved living there – a wonderful bungalow with a big garden. My aunt, uncle and cousin lived in a prefab that backed onto ours, so we had the run of both gardens. However, there were just two bedrooms, and my brother and I shared one. As we got older, my father divided the room with a curtain to give us some privacy.

When I was 12, the council built an 11-storey block of flats and four blocks of maisonettes nearby. My family was offered a two-storey, three-bedroom maisonette, and my brother and I were excited to each be getting our own bedroom. My aunt, uncle and cousin were offered a two-bedroom flat in the big block, and they were not happy at all. This was in about 1967. People were not used to living in high-rise flats yet. Although there was green space round the new blocks, we no longer had a garden and really missed that. At the prefab, we'd had trees and flowerbeds at the front and a lawn, vegetable garden and two sheds at the back.

In our early years in the new home we had some of our old neighbours, who had moved to the same estate. Somehow, probably because of the layout of the new estate and the lack of gardens, there wasn't the same sense of community. We didn't mix as much; we came home from work or school and shut the door. My aunt and uncle hated living in a high-rise block. Eventually, they managed to raise money to buy a place and moved away. We all remembered the prefabs as our best and most wonderful homes. I still dream about it.[5]

A changing landscape

At first, residents were keen on the modern flats, but poor construction and lack of management and upkeep by cash-strapped local authorities led to a gradual decline in many of the high-rise developments. The high-rises – and much other housing – were also adversely affected by economic downturns and industrial decline, such as in Sheffield in the 1970s and 1980s.

Some of the main criticisms high-rises faced were insufficient amenities and few welcoming spaces to socialise and bring up children, although that was not the case. Some high-rises fell victim to the process of 'residualisation', where the more troubled families and vulnerable tenants were the ones to be housed in the less favoured blocks. This coincided with the powerful perception that the high-rises engender anti-social behaviour.

The City of Birmingham, for example, which was blighted by slums, had embraced high-rises with gusto, making compulsory purchases in 1947 in order to provide 33,000 new homes in 'mixed developments'. Land was redeveloped in the city centre and on the outskirts, but as there was a concern about land shortage, the pressure was to build ever higher. By 1963, 85 per cent of the Council's building was high-rise (Fig 5.2). Unfortunately, one-upmanship between council leaders compromised both the planning and design of the new high-rises and, though Birmingham did manage to largely solve its housing crisis, by the early 1970s, the tide was turning. Tower blocks began to be seen as unsuitable for young families, and many of the blocks were knocked down or redeveloped.

Fig 5.2
Aerial image of Aston New Town,
Birmingham taken in 1999.
[NMR_18490_19]

Meanwhile, in Manchester, the working-class and overcrowded district of Hulme was ripe for post-war redevelopment. Slum clearance started in 1954 but stalled as new homes were not being completed quickly enough. To speed things up, the Council opted for four deck-access, six-storey crescent blocks – 924 homes in all – which made Hulme Crescents the largest social-housing scheme in Europe when it was completed in 1972 (Fig 5.3). The scheme's designers, Hugh Wilson and Lewis Womersley, opted for prefabricated concrete panels and promised 'a high quality of finish, both internally and externally... obtained because structural components, fittings and services will be manufactured and supervised under factory conditions and not subjected to climatic and other hazards of an open site'.[6] But poor construction resulted in the Crescents' flats

Fig 5.3
Aerial image of Hulme Crescents, Manchester taken in 1971.
[EAW217722]

leaking. The underfloor heating system proved to be expensive to use and resulted in both extensive condensation problems and cockroach infestations. Three years after they had moved in, some 96 per cent of the residents wanted to leave, and the only course of action was to demolish the buildings in 1994. They were replaced by conventional red-brick terraces and low-rise flats.

By the late 1960s, it was becoming apparent that the ideal of high-rise living had not materialised, although construction continued. Public opinion was turning against them, and the central-government subsidy for building high was withdrawn by 1967. Their construction came to a virtual halt in the 1970s, due in part to the collapse of Ronan Point in East London (Fig 5.4). A system-built block of 110 flats, it was assembled from prefabricated concrete panels and held

Fig 5.4
Ronan Point, East London, partially collapsed after an internal explosion in 1968.
[P_Z00450_004]

together by bolts. In 1968, a gas explosion in the kitchen in a flat on the 18th floor caused the block to partially collapse only two months after the building's opening, and resulted in the death of four people.[7] This incident, combined with a range of defects associated with system-building in other developments, irrevocably tarnished the modernists' high-rise vision for Britain. Indeed, many Conservatives wished to halt high-rise construction altogether, seeing it as 'socialist architecture'.

It is fair to say that the reality of these high-rise blocks often differed widely from the architectural ideals from which they stemmed. More often than not, architects failed to retain their influence over public housing, while local government and building contractors became increasingly concerned with high output rather than aesthetics and post-war social ideals. The financial recession of the 1970s put an end to many large-scale construction projects and, as a result, building of all types declined in the late 1970s and didn't pick up again until a decade later. By the time residential building resumed in earnest, the emphasis had moved away from the ambitious council estates of the 1960s to the construction of pitched-roofed private houses and low-rise flats.

To solve the pressing issue of failing estates, some high-rises, such as Keeling House in Bethnal Green and the Park Hill estate in Sheffield, were sold off by cash-strapped councils to private developers, which has led to significant gentrification and often the dissemination of long-established communities. Others, such as Ronan Point, have been entirely demolished. But architect-led projects demonstrate that it is possible to preserve the modernists' creations while retaining the communities within. Hillington Square estate (Fig 5.5) in King's Lynn, Norfolk – a series of 1960s five-storey concrete-frame blocks – has been renovated by Mae Architects. According to lead architect Alex Ely, the project is proof that the country's less successful social-housing estates can be rehabilitated. 'It is possible to remodel estates, affording them all the qualities of a new development whilst importantly retaining their sense of community and finding value in their original ideas', Ely said in an interview with *Dezeen*.[8] The update saw the estate lose the elevated walkways and gain separate staircases and lifts, giving each home its own direct access, which, it is hoped, will help to foster a greater sense of ownership. The flats' interiors have also been

Fig 5.5
Regeneration of the Hillington Square estate in King's Lynn, Norfolk (1967–71) began in 2015. [© Archant CM Ltd – Norfolk, 2348913]

refurbished. The fabric of Hillington Square was sound and the remodelling has allowed the architects to develop a blueprint for adapting such estates, extending their lifespan and overcoming any initial design flaws.

The prefab returns as 'mobile home'

In 1961, council-house waiting lists had reached their peak, especially in London. Moreover, standards of living were still very poor in certain areas, where it was common to see families living in bedsits with an outdoor toilet. A committee appointed by the Ministry of Housing and Local Government and led by Sir Parker Morris published an influential report on housing space standards entitled *Homes of Today and Tomorrow*. It concluded that the quality and size of social housing had to be improved and standardised. It defined space standards, determined what furniture was needed and the space required for household activities, and it imposed a flushing toilet in every dwelling.[9] Shortly after the publication of the report, the increasingly desperate housing situation forced the LCC to take emergency measures and build prefabs once again. This time, they called them 'mobile homes', but their design, their floor plans and the materials used were influenced by their older siblings, the temporary prefabs.

These new prefabs were called the Atlanta, the Terrapin and the Paladin Sun Cottage (Fig 5.6). Designed and manufactured by the company Calders in Washington, County Durham, they were equipped with all the necessary fittings, fixtures and even furniture. The Atlanta was transportable as a complete unit; after unloading, wheels, axles and springs were replaced by steel jacks

Fig 5.6
Paladin Sun Cottages were put up in London in the 1960s as temporary accommodation.
[© London Metropolitan Archives]

resting on concrete pads. The Terrapin came in two separate units that were joined together in less than an hour, while the Paladin Sun Cottages were simple timber bungalows that could be erected on pre-prepared foundations in about one hour.[10]

The three models were exhibited for public inspection in London in 1961, on the South Bank near Waterloo Bridge. People who were on social-housing waiting lists were especially encouraged to look at them. The Atlanta wasn't particularly popular – people thought it looked too much like an American caravan – but the Terrapin and the Paladin Sun Cottage had more success, and from 1962, about 200 were erected by the LCC on various sites around east and south London as temporary accommodation while new permanent homes were being constructed.

The LCC also contributed its own prefab design – the LCC Mobile Home (Fig 5.7) – designed by LCC architects in conjunction with the Timber Development Association and also manufactured by Calders. Designed to be moved from site to site if necessary, it resembled the American prefab, with a flat roof and a very similar floor plan. Adhering to the space standards set out in the Parker Morris report, it was slightly bigger than the Terrapin and the Paladin Sun Cottages and was superior to them: for example, while the Terrapin had only a thick curtain to separate the living room from the main bedroom, the LCC Mobile Home had a proper wall (Fig 5.8).

Early in 1962, local authorities started erecting the LCC Mobile Homes around Bethnal Green, Bermondsey and Elephant and Castle. Arriving in two parts, each 9ft 6in (2.9m) wide and together weighing about 8 tonnes, the LCC Mobile Home could be erected in about an hour (Fig 5.9). A flagstone base had to be prepared and a crane was used to position the two parts of the house into place. The homes were clad externally with tough asbestos panels, the floors and roof were plywood, insulated with foamed polystyrene, and the flat roof was finished with bituminous felt. The homes had an entrance hall, lounge, two bedrooms, a kitchen and a bathroom with WC and washbasin.

Fig 5.7
LCC Mobile Homes in
Kennington, London, 1970s.
[© Tom Dolan]

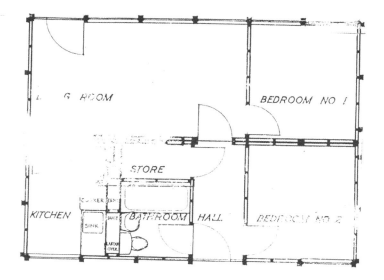

Fig 5.8
Floor plan of the LCC Mobile
Home. [© Dave Bregula]

Fig 5.9
An LCC Mobile Home arriving
on a truck. LCC mobile homes
were erected on various sites as
part of a London-wide temporary
accommodation programme
designed to alleviate the acute
housing shortage in the early
1960s. [© London Metropolitan
Archives]

Although they were designed by the LCC for use in the capital, more than 100 were also erected in Liverpool, as the city was suffering a similar housing crisis. The homes' structure meant that, in theory, they could be moved from place to place, but in practice, the cost of site preparation, services and removal meant that this option was rarely taken up, although some did find their way to Oxford and Belfast.[11]

Moving into an LCC Mobile Home

Dave Bregula

The situation in London was still very bad in the early 1960s. My mum and dad had two children at that time: my sisters were two years and six months old respectively. The LCC Mobile Home was their first offer of a home in two years. This wasn't unusual; it was done on a points system of your need. Mum and Dad got a letter about the mobile home from the Council. It said that these were temporary bungalows and it would not affect their right to a council home, but they needed to be in the mobile home for at least three years. Dad had heard that four had just been put up on Stepney High Street, so they went there to have a look. No one had moved into them yet, so Mum had a look through the letterbox into the hall. When she saw the bathroom, she said to Dad, 'Right, we'll take one!' The mobiles had an Ascot water heater and you had hot water whenever you wanted it – pure luxury.

There were 20 mobile homes in Essian Street, our street in the East End. Before the mobile homes, the street had four old houses and emergency Nissen huts had replaced houses that had been bombed during the war. In Tower Hamlets, there were more than 30 mobile-home sites with 600 plus homes; there were a few sites of older prefabs too, the Uni-Seco type in Grove Road and Globe Road. Even though they were called mobile, I would say about 80 per cent of them stayed on the site that they were first put on. Many were still up and lived in into the 1990s and some into the 2000s.[12]

More than 2,000 LCC prefabs, with a lifetime of 20 years, had been erected in the capital by the end of 1963. The LCC's Chief Architect, Hubert Bennett, was very keen on them. 'We hope to put up as many as the factory can provide', he told the *Daily Mail* on 5 November 1962. 'We have about 100 sites which cannot be used for permanent building for a few years yet. So we shall put up these homes.'

He was not the only one to like them – tenants did too (Fig 5.10). In October 1975, the story of two mothers leaving their tower-block flats to become squatters in their old LLC Mobile Homes made the *East London Advertiser* newspaper headlines. Local authorities finally allowed the families to stay in their prefabs. In fact, when permanent homes became available, some tenants of the temporary mobile homes didn't want to leave them. 'Many took the law into their own hands; council tenants left their flats to squat empty mobiles. Most of the tenants of my street – Essian Street – from the mid-1970s were squatters. The council ended up giving them rent books as they had children and would have needed emergency housing anyway', Dave Bregula recalls.

Despite the fact that such homes were only intended to last two decades, they were still occupied until the early 1990s. Some were even purchased through the Right to Buy scheme and can be seen today in Clacton-on-Sea in Essex (Fig 5.11).

After some of the unpopular high-rise estates were demolished, many tenants favoured a return to cottages with pitched roofs and gardens. The last of the New Towns – operational since 1946 to accommodate urban overspill – was Milton Keynes, which was designated in 1967. At its inception, its planning guideline instructed 'no building higher than the highest tree'.

Fig 5.10

Childhood in an LCC mobile home in Stepney in London's East End. [© Dave Bregula]

Fig 5.11

LCC mobile homes in Clacton-on-Sea, Essex, now used as holiday homes. [© Dave Bregula]

6 | Building the future

After the social experiment of the high-rises, prefabrication was regarded with scepticism by the public, who associated it with impermanence and poor quality. But prefabrication didn't totally disappear, and elements of it continued to be used in the building industry to a greater or lesser extent. 'Traditionally' built houses incorporate, for example, mass-produced plastic window frames, factory-made precast floors and prefabricated roof panels. This, architects say, is the future of the house-building industry: the construction of homes is quicker and requires fewer skilled workers, while consumers get a house that looks no different from a traditional one. Prefabrication has been granted a new name and is now more often referred to in terms of Modern Methods of Construction. Meanwhile, its image – at least in the private building sector – is being resuscitated by TV programmes such as *Grand Designs*.

Margaret Thatcher's Right to Buy policy (introduced in 1980) reduced social housing stock, and the sharp drop in subsidies put a stop to the building of new schemes. The city slums may be gone, but what remains is an acute housing shortage. Today's public sector provides just 20 per cent of all houses built.[1] The charity Shelter estimates that 250,000 homes a year, half of them 'affordable', need to be built in England if the crisis is to be addressed. Yet 2015 saw only 135,050 new homes – a little more than half of what is needed. 'Fewer houses are being built, tens of thousands of families are living in temporary accommodation, house prices continue to rise, pushing more people into private renting, and conditions in many rented homes are as bad as we've seen in decades', Shelter's Chief Executive, Campbell Robb, told *The Guardian* newspaper.[2]

Today, politicians are grappling for a solution, and suggestions range from building more New Towns, releasing green-belt land and building higher again. In 2007, Gordon Brown planned several 'eco-towns', to be spread mostly around the south-east, but apart from one built in Bicester, these remain largely in the planning stages. Both Conservatives and Liberal Democrats have proposed building new garden cities to take the pressure off London.[3]

Modular social housing

The end of the 1990s saw a tentative re-evaluation of prefabrication, when politicians yet again flirted with it as a solution to the housing problem. In 1998, Lord Egan published 'Rethinking Construction', a report that concluded that factory-built housing is the future. The Labour government of 2005–10 recognised the potential of prefabrication for the social-housing sector because of its faster construction times and hoped it would kick-start the sluggish rates of house building.

In London, the Peabody Trust, one of the largest social landlords in the capital, commissioned Murray Grove (Fig 6.1), an affordable-housing development consisting of 30 one- and two-bedroom apartments for key workers (who often do not earn enough to get on the property ladder). The style of the

Fig 6.1 (opposite)
Murray Grove, an example of largely prefabricated modern housing, completed in 1999.
[© Selim Korycki]

Fig 6.5
The world's only certified green-bamboo prefab, manufactured away from the building site, usually in standard sections that are easy to ship and fast to assemble. [Courtesy of Bamboo Living Homes]

Fig 6.6
A tiny mobile house in Portland, Oregon. [By Tammy (Weekend with Dee), licensed for reuse under creativecommons.org/licenses/by/2.0, via Wikimedia Commons. Taken from https://commons.wikimedia.org/wiki/File:Tiny_house,_Portland.jpg]

Prefabs as emergency housing

As the world tackles increasing migration, whether through conflict or natural disasters, it has made sense to invest in prefabricated solutions to alleviate suffering. Large firms such as IKEA have responded by developing products such as the flat-pack home Better Shelter (Fig 6.7), which is particularly ingenious. More than 10,000 of these emergency homes were sent all over the world during the summer of 2015 following the exodus from Syria. The shelters, made from lightweight polymer panels laminated with thermal insulation, arrive on site in cardboard boxes and can be assembled in a few hours without tools, following an illustrated manual. Intended to house five people each, they have windows, ventilation, a lockable door and a solar panel linking to an LED light and mobile-phone charger. Each shelter costs £773 and can last for about three years. IKEA partnered with the United Nations High Committee for Refugees, which has described the shelters as a 'ground-breaking example of democratic design' that will bring people safety and dignity.[15] IKEA is planning to produce thousands more shelters over the coming years.

Fig 6.7

Ikea's flat-packed Better Shelter unit. [Courtesy of Better Shelter]

Can prefabrication be the solution again?

The failure of successive governments to build the homes that Britain needs is the main cause of today's social housing crisis. The political, social and economic contexts have, of course, changed since the end of the Second World War. The Temporary Housing Programme was an exceptional initiative, decided on and implemented by a united government on a national scale, and the concerted house-building efforts in the 1950s and 1960s saw millions lifted out of poverty and slum housing. Such national housing schemes are unlikely to happen again because of the lack of available land in cities and the lack of political will and sense of urgency. Local councils have lost much of their affordable housing stock and are no longer in a position to build the required number of new homes.

While out-and-out prefabricated homes, such as Germany's Huf Haus and Japan's Muji hut, are considered to be aspirational, prefabrication is still often associated, in the UK, with post-war austerity and impermanence. The reasons are manifold: lack of architectural and social acceptance, not enough suitable and plentiful materials to develop new building methods and not enough champions of the medium. However, having experienced a marked decline in the 1970s, the image of prefabrication is recuperating: today prefabrication often means eco-friendly homes that are cleaner and cheaper to build. What's more, as land becomes increasingly scarce, architects are thinking about how prefabrication can be used to slot houses into small spaces in cities, where no traditionally built home could otherwise fit. Whether the UK construction industry will ever see fully prefabricated housing as a viable alternative remains to be seen, but history has shown that prefabricated homes can and do come to the rescue when they're needed most.

7 | Postscript

But where are the temporary post-war prefabs today? 'These temporary homes... are likely to be a familiar part of the English scene for some years to come', proclaimed the *Illustrated London News* on 3 November 1945. And the newspaper was not wrong. Although built to last just a decade, many of them survived far beyond their intended lifespan, mostly thanks to improvements by residents, most of whom were intensely house proud. In the end, of the half a million promised by Churchill, only 156,623 had materialised by the time the Temporary Housing Programme was wound down in 1949.[1]

Although modest to the modern eye and by no means perfect, these temporary prefabs really did change people's lives by giving them the opportunity to be masters of their very own detached homes – their 'little castles'. The tenants considered themselves lucky, and the prefabs were a testament to the will to make life better for people after the trials of the Second World War. But the modernist dream of homes rolling off the production line came at a price: the average cost of a prefab was far more than the original estimate of about £1,250. Despite this, they provided shelter that was quick to build and answered most people's needs, often going far beyond their expectations.

The social coherence that existed in the prefab estates stemmed from the fact that people had a shared experience of the war and were, more often than not, starting from scratch. Some were lucky enough to be able to return to their original neighbourhoods, thus retaining all-important familial and social ties. Many of the bombed-out families on the Isle of Dogs, for example, returned to the area to live in temporary prefab homes.

At first, the temporary prefabs – which were either very different from anything that people had seen before or, conversely, were seen as far too similar to the type of shelters that soldiers had experienced during the war – were somewhat misunderstood, but they soon became aspirational and played a big part in people's social mobility. Residents were aware that whatever council housing they might be allocated in the future, it was unlikely that it would be a detached home with plentiful outdoor space and like-minded neighbours.

Jim Blackender (Fig 7.1), an ex-resident who fought to save the Excalibur Estate in Lewisham from demolition, recalls: 'Here, you have a two-bedroom detached property, and unless you have lots of money, you're never going to get that back again. It was something we were fortunate enough to have as council tenants. Once they're gone, they're gone forever; you're never going to get back to a place like that.'[2]

Tenants worked hard to improve their prefabs and often petitioned councils to add cladding to make their homes warmer and to extend their lifespans. This is what happened at Excalibur; tenants asked Lewisham Council for funding, but due to various delays, only 50 out of 186 prefabs on the estate received it.

Fig 7.1
Jim Blackender, ex-resident of the Excalibur Estate, outside his prefab home. [© Elisabeth Blanchet]

Listing post-war prefabs

In the early 1990s, when more and more of the post-war temporary prefabs were being pulled down, English Heritage (now Historic England) considered listing a selection. Historian Julian Holder suggested listing each type from the Temporary Housing Programme. 'Where good examples do occur, particular attention should be paid to the quality and completeness of the fixtures and fittings. The difference within each type should also be considered, together with the possibility of identifying early prototypes', he wrote in a survey for English Heritage in 1991.[3] As a result, Grade II status was given to 16 Phoenix prefabs on Wake Green Road, in Moseley, Birmingham, in 1998 (Fig 7.2). In 2007, two pairs of Swedish timber-frame houses in Spittlerush Lane, Doncaster, were granted Grade II listing, and in 2009, after the residents of the Excalibur Estate (Fig 7.3) tried, unsuccessfully, to have the estate listed as a conservation area, just six of 186 Uni-Secos were given Grade II status. Emily Gee, Head of Listing Advice at Historic England explains:

These six prefabs have retained many of their original features, such as doors and windows. They are of special interest as part of the largest surviving post-war prefab estate in England and present a unique example of prefab estate planning on a large scale. These six prefabs present the most historic and architectural interest for the way they reflect this important period in British history.[4]

Fig 7.2

Phoenix prefabs in Wake Green Road, Moseley. Sixteen were Grade II listed by English Heritage (now Historic England) in 1998. [© Elisabeth Blanchet]

Regeneration projects and campaigns

The temporary prefabs were so popular that residents often had to tussle with
local authorities to keep their homes (Fig 7.4). It is estimated that more than
10,000 prefabs remained in use in London as late as 1975.[5] In the 1960s and
1970s, the temporary prefabs were mainly replaced with maisonettes and tower
blocks, and some with other prefabs, such as the LLC Mobile Homes. Later, in
the 1990s and 2000s, prefab estates were replaced with bungalows or low-rise

"CAN'T GET HIM TO MOVE OUT OF IT - HE SAYS IT REMINDS HIM OF OUR OLD PREFAB!"

maisonettes built using traditional materials. In order to increase population density, homes became smaller and garden sizes were reduced or disappeared altogether.

The most effective regeneration projects were the ones where residents were consulted from the start. In Newport, where 640 Arcon Mark Vs were built in 1946, residents were given the choice in 2001 between keeping their old prefabs or opting for new brick bungalows on the same estate (Fig 7.5). The Arcon Mark Vs had reached the end of their lives. If the residents went for the new bungalow, they could choose between four different layouts, which were as similar as possible to the old prefabs. Although the residents were very attached to their old prefabs, almost everyone chose to live in a new bungalow. Fifteen years after the regeneration programme started, only three prefabs are still standing.

In Old Brampton in Derbyshire, where around 50 Tarrans were built in 1946 (Fig 7.6), residents were not offered the choice to remain in their prefabs. However, the regeneration projects were led by Rykneld Homes and the North Derbyshire Council in a participative way. Residents were involved in the decision-making and the design of the new bungalows and they could choose where they would be rehoused on the estate. Moreover, Rykneld Homes managed to rehouse people straight away from their old Tarrans into new bungalows without having to move them into temporary accommodation while their new homes were being built.

Fig 7.5

An ex-prefab resident in her new bungalow, Newport. [© Elisabeth Blanchet]

In 2002, the campaign by Alan Mason and his neighbours in Redditch, Worcestershire, saved 30 BL8 prefabs from being pulled down by the local authorities (Fig 7.7). Redditch Borough Council estimated that they were too costly to modernise and intended to replace the prefabs with new homes. The residents led a high-profile campaign for months, threatening to chain themselves to their prefabs' sinks and baths. Redditch councillors capitulated, concluding that the prefabs needed minimal repairs and could stay.

In 2013, in Ipswich, where there are still 142 Tarran prefabs in the Inverness Road area (Fig 7.8), Conservative Councillor Judy Terry caused serious concern among the residents when she suggested the prefabs should be demolished and the area redeveloped. After a vote, residents chose to keep their prefabs. 'People love their homes in that part of the town and while we are not guaranteeing they will always be there, it seems sensible to carry out the work to extend their lives at this time. We are building new homes in other parts of the town. It doesn't seem sensible to start knocking down those homes at this stage', John Mowles, the borough councillor with responsibility for housing, told the *Ipswich Star*.[6] As a consequence, more than £600,000 was allocated to improve the prefabs.

The treatment of prefab tenants at the Excalibur Estate has been less cordial. Since the 1970s, local authorities had made several attempts to regenerate the land. The residents tried to save the estate, but a vote to 'regenerate' it in 2010 actually meant that the homes would be knocked down: although tenants had been promised that they would be allocated new homes on the rebuilt estate, they saw their prefabs being decanted one by one, while they themselves were rehoused in different parts of the borough and beyond. The community was broken up and the former homes now stand empty and boarded up.

Fig 7.7
In 2002, Alan Mason, who later became the Mayor of Redditch, led the successful campaign to save 30 BL8 bungalows from demolition. [© Elisabeth Blanchet]

Fig 7.8
With 142 prefabs on and around Inverness Road, Ipswich has the UK's largest remaining prefab estate. [© Elisabeth Blanchet]

Rethinking conservation and regeneration

Keeping true to the post-war spirit of make-do-and-mend, some temporary prefabs have found a new lease of life as sailing clubhouses (Fig 7.9), buildings on farms, a tea house in a transport museum, garages and workshops and even a pub (The Arches, in Great Yarmouth, Norfolk).

In Birmingham, a project is underway to transform 16 listed prefabs into holiday lets, guaranteeing them a longer life. Residents will be able to stay in their prefabs while three or four empty ones will be turned into holiday bungalows. The idea was inspired by Cultybraggan Camp, in Comrie, Scotland, which was originally constructed as a PoW camp in 1941 and then used as an army base for 50 years before being put up for sale with its 80 Nissen huts, some of which are now listed by Historic Scotland (Fig 7.10). Comrie Development Trust purchased the 40-acre (16ha) camp in 2007 and has since been developing it for a range of uses, including heritage tours, events, education, allotments, businesses, a community orchard and local voluntary organisations.[7]

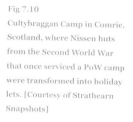

Fig 7.9
A UK100 prefab, now being used by a sailing club in Snettisham, Norfolk. [© Peter Gale]

Fig 7.10
Cultybraggan Camp in Comrie, Scotland, where Nissen huts from the Second World War that once serviced a PoW camp were transformed into holiday lets. [Courtesy of Strathearn Snapshots]

Living history

Temporary prefabs can also be found in museums. Refurbished and displaying period furniture and objects, their interiors show visitors how comfortable, modern and very well designed they really were. Kitchens are particularly fascinating in terms of fittings and fixtures. Different types of prefabs can be seen: an AIROH B2 in St Fagans National Museum of History in Cardiff (Fig 7.11), a Universal at the Chiltern Open Air Museum (Fig 7.12), Arcon Mark Vs at the Avoncroft Museum of Historic Buildings in Bromsgrove (Fig 7.13) and at the Rural Life Centre in Farnham (Fig 7.14), and a Tarran at the Eden Camp Modern History Theme Museum in Malton, North Yorkshire.

Fig 7.11
This was one of 40 such prefabs that were built in Llandinam Crescent in 1948. It now resides in St Fagans National Museum of History, Wales. [© Elisabeth Blanchet]

Fig 7.12
The Universal House Mark 3 prefab at the Chiltern Open Air Museum was one of 46 on the Finch Lane Estate in Amersham, Buckinghamshire. It has been used for filming various television programmes, including *Call the Midwife*. [© David Willis]

Fig 7.13
Arcon Mark V Prefab at the
Avoncroft Museum of Historic
Buildings in Bromsgrove,
Worcestershire. [© Elisabeth
Blanchet]

Fig 7.14
The Arcon Mark V at the Rural
Life Centre in Farnham, Surrey,
dates from about 1947. In 2002, it
was fitted out with parts obtained
from five of the hundreds of
similar buildings in Bristol that
were being demolished by the
local authority. [© Elisabeth
Blanchet]

The Moving Prefab Museum and Archive was inspired by photographer and author Elisabeth Blanchet's documenting of prefabs, their current and ex-residents and their stories. A photography exhibition in 2013 was followed by guided tours and tea parties, at which former residents shared their stories. These activities culminated in a temporary museum in a vacant prefab on the Excalibur Estate. During the museum's seven-month residency from March to October 2014, there was a programme of activities, including expert guest talks, a VE day event, tours, workshops and tea parties. Volunteers were from the estate's community, artists and amateur historians. The Prefab Museum worked with local community groups, schools, history societies and interest groups from across the UK. Nearly 5,000 people visited the museum and its archive can now be found online.

Prefabs from this era can also be found abroad. In France, for example, 154,000 prefabs were erected in the north of France, where they were used to help with the post-war housing crisis. There were different types of prefabs but the most popular was the UK100: like Britain, France received 8,000 of them from the USA. The organisation Memoire de Soye has re-assembled an original UK 100, near Lorient, in Brittany, where post-war memories are brought vividly to life (Fig 7.15)

Fig 7.15

A UK100 re-assembled and transformed into a museum by Mémoire de Soye, Ploemeur, France, 2015. [© Elisabeth Blanchet]

Prefabs in films and art

There is a growing nostalgia around temporary prefabs. They regularly crop up on television and can be seen in the ITV drama *Foyle's War* and BBC dramas *Call The Midwife* and *WPC 56*. The Excalibur Estate was used many times as a film set for *Only Fools and Horses* (Fig 7.16) and for music videos. Prefabs also inspired an artistic response. London Artist Bobby Baker created 'An Edible Family in a Mobile Home' (Fig 7.17), a life-size installation of an 'edible' family made from cake in a LCC Mobile Home that she was lent by Acme Housing Association in Stepney Green in 1976.[8]

Fig 7.16

Shooting an episode of *Only Fools and Horses* at the Excalibur Estate, Catford. [© David Miller]

Fig 7.17

'An Edible Family in a Mobile Home' by Bobby Baker, 1976, photographed in front of a LCC Mobile Home in East London. [© Andrew Whittuck]

Appendix:
List of temporary prefabs

With the help of local historians and prefab enthusiasts, the authors have been collating an interactive digital resource to document all locations of temporary prefabs past and present in the UK. The following is a chronological list of the principle types of temporary prefabs. For an evolving digital map see: https://www.prefabmuseum.uk

Phoenix (Fig A.1)
Date: 1930s
Designer: John Laing, McAlpine and Henry Boot Ltd
Unit cost: £1,200
Total cost: £2,914,000
Number manufactured: 2,428
Location: All over Britain.
Main materials used: Timber frame with asbestos cladding
Specificities: Very similar to the Uni-Seco but with a pitched roof.
Remaining examples: Seventeen survive in good condition on Wake Green Road, Moseley, Birmingham, 16 of which were listed in 1998 by Historic England.

Tarran Bungalow (Fig A.2)
Date: Late 1930s, early 1940s
Designer: Robert Tarran from Tarran Industries of Hull (and also Edinburgh, Leeds and Dundee).
Costs (there were three types of Tarran bungalows):
MK2: £1,022 per unit (1,015 manufactured), total cost £1,037,000
MK3: £1,147 per unit (11,000 manufactured), total cost £12,617,000
MK4: £1,126 per unit (6,999 manufactured), total cost £7,881,000
Total number manufactured: 19,014
Location: All over Britain but mainly in the north and east of England
Main material used: Concrete
Specificities: The Tarran bungalow design was almost identical to the Uni-Seco, with the exception of the roof, which in the Tarran was traditionally pitched, made of asbestos concrete and clad on the outside with concrete panels. This made the Tarrans particularly heavy (14 tons each) and probably explains why they were erected mainly in the north, close to the factory that manufactured them.
Remaining examples: There is an estate of 142 Tarrans still occupied in Ipswich (Inverness Road). Others remain, mainly in 'pockets' of a few to about 50, in North Derbyshire and Yorkshire. (For more information on their location, refer to The Prefab Museum's map.)

Supporters

The names listed below are of readers who have pledged their support and helped make this book happen. If you'd like to join them, visit www.unbound.co.uk.

Myles Albon-Crouch
Neil Anderson
Christine Antonini
Adrian Armishaw
Ben Austwick
Mary Barber
Charles Bowyer
Jim Brettell
Matt Bruce
Clare Butler
Paul Clarke
Diana Cochrane
Patricia Coker
Katya Colley
Kate Collis
Mark Cooper
Robert Cox
Sergio da Silva
Richard Davies
David Elliott
Mike Evans
Gabrielle Fonseca Johnson
Mark Fox
Sergei Grachev
Dorothy Halfhide
Leslie Hardy

Chris Harry
David Heath
Scott Hedges
Charles Horsey
John Hudson
Barbara Hungin
Joseph Hungin
Kiran Hungin
Heather Hyams
Andrew Johnson
Stephen Johnson
Artemy Kalinovsky
Marina Kamenskaya
Masha Karp
Catriona Kelly
Angela Kenrick
Dan Kieran
Jon Lawrence
Robert Leach
Ian Lee
Mick Lemmerman
Roy Levien
Tom Long
Brian Mahoney
Sam Manning
Ian Mansfield
Lee Melin
James Mewis
John Mitchinson
Chris Moxey
Lance Moxon
Carlo Navato
David Neill

Ray Newman
Hazel Nicholson
Doreen O'Rourke
Michael Paley
Clare Palmer
James Palmer
Emily Petretta
Jane Petrie
Ian Pleace
Justin Pollard
Alison Porter
Julian Porter
Tony Presland
Robert Pugsley
Bill Richards
Amy Richardson
Anne Roache
Daniel Robertson
Andrew Rodger
Alla Rubitel
Brian Screaton
Vivienne Snelus
Martin Snow
Alison Steele
Daniel Stilwell
Peter Leslie Stone
Steve Sykes
Elena Varshavskaya
Vicky Walker
Miranda Whiting
Giles Williams
Alexander Zhuravlyov
Nana Zhvitiashvili